Find Out About It!

By Gill Stacey

Contents

Writing a Research Report

Your teacher has asked you to write a report. What do you do? This book will help you to plan your work and find the right information. It will also help you write and present your report.

I'm Oscar Owl. I'll help you at each step of writing your report.

The Story of the Titanic

Titanic   by Frank Sloan

World Book Encyclopedia

Eyewitness Guides: Titanic

Famous Shipwrecks

The History of Transport

The Atlas of Shipwrecks & Treasures

STEP 1 Plan Your Work

Before you start, check how long the report should be and when it is due. For example, you might have about three weeks to write a report. Then make a timetable to keep you on track.

How to Plan Your Work

1 List each step in writing your report. (See the timetable opposite.)

2 Divide up the time that you have for the whole project and set a date, or deadline, to finish each step. Finding information will probably take the most time.

3 Write your deadlines on the timetable.

4 Check your timetable every day to make sure that you're on track.

My Report Timetable

Day		Step	Done
Thu	1	Choose a topic.	☐
Fri	2	Find information. Take notes.	☐
Sat	3		☐
Sun	4		☐
Mon	5		☐
Tue	6		☐
Wed	7		☐
Thu	8	Organize notes. Make an outline.	☐
Fri	9		☐
Sat	10		☐
Sun	11		☐
Mon	12	Write the report.	☐
Tue	13		☐
Wed	14		☐
Thu	15		☐
Fri	16	Practise presenting the report.	☐
Sat	17		☐
Sun	18		☐
Mon	19	Present the report.	☐

STEP 2 Choose a Topic

You have been asked to write a report on the history of transport. The history of transport is a large topic. It covers hundreds of years and there are many kinds of transport, such as cars, boats, planes and trains. Researching a topic like this could take years, so you will need to narrow it down.

How to Choose a Topic

1 Write down as many ideas that you can think of about the topic. This is called brainstorming.

2 Now narrow down your list. Cross out topics that are too general for one report or too narrow. Cross out any ideas that don't interest you or are not related to your topic.

3 Circle the topic that you would like to know more about.

History of Transport :
Topic Ideas

~~The history of ships and boats~~
Too broad – it would take me
a year to write all that.

~~How to sail a boat~~
I'd like to know this, but it
doesn't fit the assignment.

⟨The Titanic⟩

The Titanic was a famous ship
that sank. Why did it sink?
I'd like to know more about it.

4 Think about what you want to know about your topic and ask questions to help you gather the facts. Use words such as *who*, *what*, *when*, *where*, *why* and *how* to form your questions.

5 Write your questions on a sheet of paper. Use your questions as a checklist while you research to be sure you cover all the important facts.

Titanic Questions

What was the <u>Titanic</u>?

How was the <u>Titanic</u> different from other ships?

Who was on the ship? Who built it?

When did it sink?

Why did it sink?

What did people learn from the disaster?

Why do we still remember it today?

The *Titanic*

The sinking of the *Titanic* was one of the most famous transport disasters. The ship hit an iceberg when sailing from Southampton to New York, USA. The accident happened on 14th April 1912.

newspaper reports and photos from the time

STEP 3 Find Information

Now it's time to find out more about your topic. Remember that an interesting report presents information from different **sources**. Look for information in books, magazines, newspapers, **encyclopedias**, on the internet and by watching educational programmes on television.

Use an Encyclopedia

Encyclopedia articles give basic facts, so they are a good place to start your research. Most encyclopedias have a series of books or volumes. Topics are listed in alphabetical order.

How to Use an Encyclopedia

1 Make a list of keywords related to your topic.

2 Look for your keywords in the correct volume of the encyclopedia. Each volume will have a number or range of letters to guide you.

3 Use the **guide words** at the top of each page to find your topic. Then use the **entry words** on the page to find the article.

Research Tip

Keywords are important words related to your topic. For example, you might use keywords such as *Titanic*, *ships* and *shipwrecks* when researching the *Titanic*.

4 Check the list of related topics at the end of the article to see if they lead you to more information.

5 Most **reference books** cannot be taken out of a library. Use small sticky notes to mark the pages you want to take notes from later.

Encyclopedia Article

guide word

entry word

Titanic

The *Titanic* was a floating hotel. First-class passengers paid a lot of money to travel in complete luxury.

On the morning of 10th April 1912 nearly 2,000 passengers boarded the *Titanic*, which was on its first sea voyage from Southampton, England, to New York. The ship could carry up to 3,547 passengers and crew. No expense was spared in making the *Titanic* and it was the grandest ship at that time. Everything on board was brand new or specially made for the ship; everything was designed to make the passengers comfortable and to entertain them during the voyage. The *Titanic's* builders claimed the ship was "virtually unsinkable" and most people believed there was no chance that the ship would sink. However, on 14th April 1912 the *Titanic* collided with an iceberg in the Atlantic Ocean. In less than three hours the ship sank. In total, 1,490 passengers died.

Model of the *Titanic*

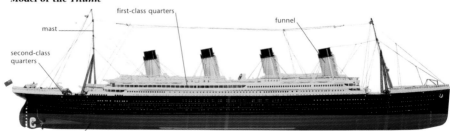

first-class quarters

funnel

mast

second-class quarters

third-class quarters

Iceberg
Icebergs are large pieces of ice that have detached from glaciers in the ocean. Icebergs drift slowly in the ocean and can be dangerous for ships.

Dinner plates found on the wreck.   restored plate

9

Use the Library

Most libraries have hundreds of books, so finding information on your topic might seem difficult. However, non-fiction books are organized by a system of numbers called the **Dewey Decimal System**. Each book has its own number that you can find in the **card catalogue**. This lists books by the subject, author and title.

Subject Card

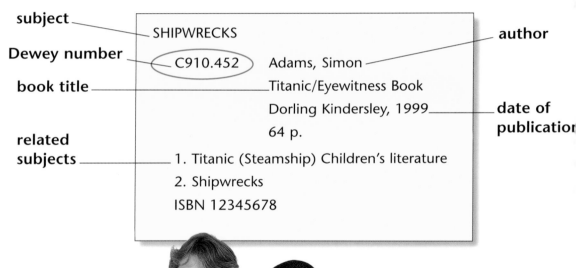

subject — SHIPWRECKS

author

Dewey number — C910.452   Adams, Simon — author

book title — Titanic/Eyewitness Book

Dorling Kindersley, 1999 — date of publication

64 p.

related subjects — 1. Titanic (Steamship) Children's literature

2. Shipwrecks

ISBN 12345678

Research Tip

Some card catalogues are printed on index cards and some are on computers. They are organized in the same way. If you need help using the card catalogue, ask a librarian.

How to Use a Card Catalogue

1. Use your keywords to look for subject cards in the card catalogue. If you are using a computer catalogue, then select the subject search and enter one or two keywords.

2. Find the **Dewey number** of the book. This number tells you where to find the book. The letter C stands for child, meaning it will be in the children's section.

3. Write down the Dewey numbers and titles of the books you want to find.

4. Use the Dewey number to find each book on the shelves. Most libraries have signs on the shelves that guide you to a range of numbers, such as 0–100. Find the range that includes your Dewey numbers and select your books.

5. Sign out your books with your library card.

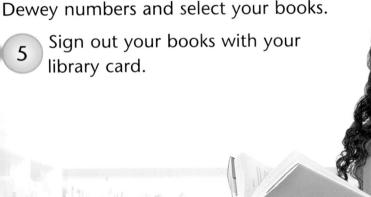

Search the Internet

Information for your report is at your fingertips. Sit down at a computer and search the internet. If you don't have a computer, then ask the librarian to help you connect to the internet in the library.

How to Search the Internet

1 Open the **browser** by clicking on it with your mouse.

2 Go to the box labelled *Address* on your browser and type in the name of a **search engine** to find websites related to your topic. Ask a librarian to suggest a good search engine.

Back   Forward   Stop   Refresh

@ http:

address box

3 Now type one or two of your keywords in the *Search* box and click on *Enter* or *Return*. A list of websites with brief descriptions will appear on your screen.

Research Tip

Not all websites have good information. Ask a librarian, a teacher or another adult to suggest some good sites. Make sure you have the correct spellings of the web addresses.

4 Read the descriptions and click on a website that looks promising.

5 Scan the page to see if the article has information you need. Print out any useful pages and write down the web addresses.

6 Click on the arrow or *Back* button to return to the search engine results to try other websites.

7 Read the pages you printed. Use a highlighter to mark the important information or take notes.

In 1912 most people got information about the *Titanic* by reading newspapers.

Today many people get their information from the internet.

Take Notes

Once you have found all your information, it's time to take notes. Index cards are good for note-taking. Do not copy information word for word. Use your own words.

How to Take Notes

1. Write your research questions at the top of your index cards and then see how your sources answer the questions.

2. Write facts and details on the index cards to answer each question. You don't need to write in complete sentences.

3. Record where you found the information on each card. Include the author, title, publisher and date of publication for books and articles. Write down the web addresses and the authors of websites.

4. Keep taking notes until you have enough facts to write your report. You can have more than one index card for each question.

How was the Titanic different from other ships?

- the largest ship of its time
- thought to be unsinkable
- had many elegant rooms and other features
- was one of the first ships to have a gym and a swimming pool

Sloan, Frank: <u>Titanic</u>. Raintree Steck-Vaughn, 1998.

The *Titanic* had a grand staircase.

Why did the Titanic sink?

- going too fast in the icy water
- hit an iceberg
- iceberg caused cracks and holes in the ship
- water flooded too many compartments in the bottom of the ship

World Book Encyclopedia, "Titanic". World Book Inc, 2002.

The *Titanic* hit an iceberg in the North Atlantic Ocean.

Make an Outline

By now you will have information from several different sources. Organize your information before you start writing. Follow these steps to prepare an outline of your report.

How to Make an Outline

1. Organize your index cards into groups of related questions. Each pile of cards represents a main idea.

2. Begin your outline with the **Roman numeral** I and label it *Introduction*.

3. Write each main idea beside another Roman numeral (II, III and so on). Leave plenty of space between each one.

4. Add details that support your main ideas. Label each detail by using capital letters *A, B, C* and so on. Use *1, 2* and *3* to number any information that you add under the *A, B* or *C* headings. (See page 17.)

5. Read your outline to see if the order of the information makes sense. Rearrange the sections if you need to.

6. Add one last Roman numeral and label it *Conclusion*.

le of
per

The Titanic

I. Introduction

troduction
belled as "I"

    A. What the Titanic was

    B. Why it is famous

II. Facts about the Titanic

A photo of the Titanic from 1912.

    A. Why it was built

    B. What was special about it?

        1. People thought it was unsinkable

        2. Most luxurious ship built at that time

        3. Had many rich and famous passengers

ain events

III. What happened?

    A. Hit an iceberg

    B. Why it sank

    C. How people got off the ship

    D. Why so many died

IV. The wreck

    A. When it was found

st Roman
umeral is
Conclusion"

    B. What we learned

V. Conclusion

Only 700 passengers, mostly women and children, boarded lifeboats and were saved.

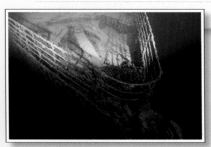

The bow of the Titanic has layers of rust from years of being under water.

STEP 5 Write Your Report

You've organized your information, so you're finally ready to write. Use your notes and your outline to guide you while you write your report.

How to Write Your Report

1. Review your index cards and outline. Think about who will read your report.

2. Begin your report with an *Introduction* that tells your readers what your report is about and grabs their interest.

3. Write the main text of your report. Use your outline to write a paragraph for each main idea and use your index cards to fill in any missing details.

4. End your report with a *Conclusion*. Remind your readers what you think is most important about your topic.

itle ————————————— **The <u>Titanic</u>**

ntroduction ————— The <u>Titanic</u> was one of the most famous ships that was ever built. People remember the <u>Titanic</u> because it sank on its first voyage. This disaster shocked the world.

main text ————— On 14th April 1912 crew members aboard the <u>Titanic</u> saw a huge iceberg. They tried to turn the ship, but it was too big. It was going too fast so it hit the iceberg. Holes were torn in the ship's side and the ship began to fill with water. Only a few hours later the <u>Titanic</u> sank.

conclusion ————— Everyone thought that the <u>Titanic</u> was unsinkable, so they were shocked when it sank. It was a sad lesson, but the <u>Titanic</u> disaster taught people how to travel more safely by ship. People will always remember the <u>Titanic</u>.

This activity is continued on page 20.

5 Revise your draft. Make sure that:
  • the report is the right length
  • the organization makes sense
  • your questions are answered
  • all the information relates to the topic.

6 Edit and polish your report by checking your spelling, capitalization, grammar and punctuation so you can correct any mistakes.

Remember to check your spelling on the computer or in a dictionary.

Bibliography

Adams, Simon, <u>Eyewitness Guides: Titanic</u>. London: Dorling Kindersley, 1999.

Kamuda, Edward S, "Titanic: Past and Present." The Titanic Historical Society, Inc. <u>http://www.titanic1org.articles</u>

Sloan, Frank, <u>Titanic</u>. Austin: Raintree Steck-Vaughn, 1998.

"Titanic", <u>World Book Encyclopedia</u>: Chicago: World Book Inc, 2002.

7 List the **sources** that you used in alphabetical order on a separate sheet of paper. (Use the information that you recorded while taking notes.) This is called a bibliography.

8 Make a cover and add illustrations. Number the pages and attach them together, putting the bibliography at the end.

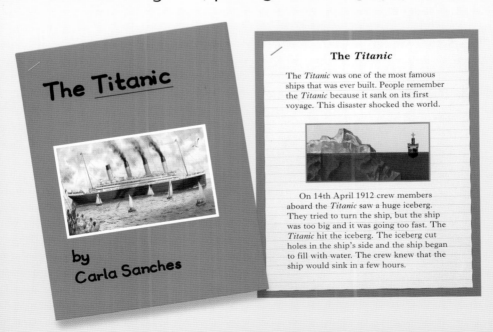

The Titanic
by Carla Sanches

The _Titanic_

The _Titanic_ was one of the most famous ships that was ever built. People remember the _Titanic_ because it sank on its first voyage. This disaster shocked the world.

On 14th April 1912 crew members aboard the _Titanic_ saw a huge iceberg. They tried to turn the ship, but the ship was too big and it was going too fast. The _Titanic_ hit the iceberg. The iceberg cut holes in the ship's side and the ship began to fill with water. The crew knew that the ship would sink in a few hours.

STEP 6 Present Your Report

If you followed the steps in this book, you've done a fine job writing your report. Now all you have left to do is present it in class. Practise your presentation with these steps and relax.

How to Prepare Your Presentation

1. Read your report aloud or silently several times.

2. Underline or highlight the main ideas in your report so you can focus on the most important information.

3. Stand in front of a mirror and practise your presentation aloud. Imagine speaking naturally and clearly to your audience.

4. Practise in front of an audience, such as a friend or a parent. Be sure not to hold your report in front of your face.

Now you're ready to present your report to your class.

Glossary

browser	a computer program that allows people to view websites
card catalogue	an alphabetical listing of the books in a library; it organizes books by subject, title and author
Dewey Decimal System	a system of numbers that organizes non-fiction books by subject
Dewey number	a number on a library book that tells people where to find that book on the shelves
encyclopedias	books or sets of books that give information on different subjects
entry words	words in bold, usually in alphabetical order, that tell you the subjects or articles on a page in a reference book
guide words	words at the top of a page in a reference book that give the first or last entry on the page
reference books	books with organized information on different subjects, such as encyclopedias and dictionaries
Roman numerals	letters of the Roman alphabet that are used as numbers
search engine	software used to gather information from the internet
sources	books, newspapers, magazines and websites used to find information

Index